William H. Willimon

FEAR OF THE OTHER

NO FEAR IN LOVE

LEADER GUIDE

by Erin M. Hawkins

Nashville

FEAR OF THE OTHER LEADER GUIDE:
NO FEAR IN LOVE

This book is printed on acid-free paper.

ISBN: 978-1-5018-5730-0

17 18 19 20 21 22 23 24 25 26—10 9 8 7 6 5 4 3 2 1

MANUFACTURED IN THE UNITED STATES OF AMERICA

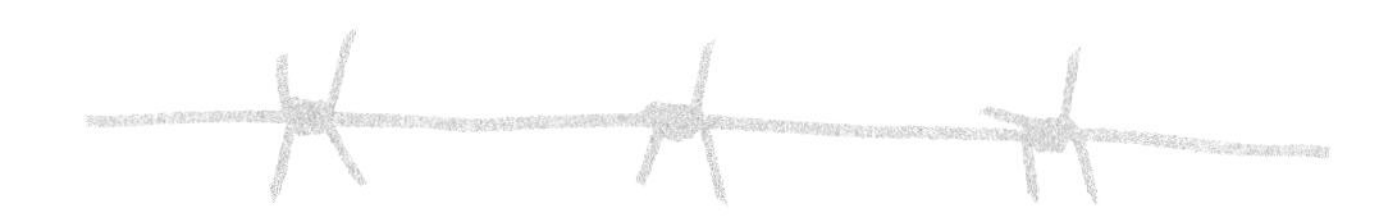

CONTENTS

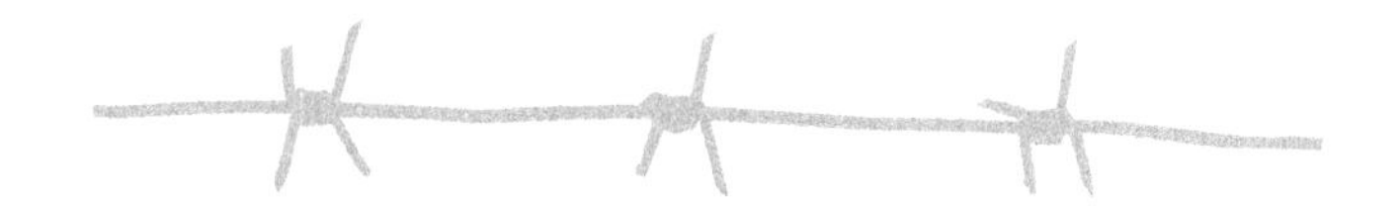

HOW TO USE THIS GUIDE

Fear of the Other is a subject whose time has come given the divided nature of relationships in the church and world today. Thank you for saying yes to facilitating a process in which participants through study and dialogue can explore their histories and beliefs in light of their commitment to be disciples of Jesus Christ. As a facilitator, you play a key role in the weekly classroom sessions, which are a critical component of the study's overall experience. Your guidance will shape the interactions between the participants and nurture the impact this study has on their lives.

This is a five-week study that encourages participants to explore who they consider the Other to be in their lives and communities and begin regarding the Other from a Christian perspective. By the end of the study, your participants will be able to

- identify the Other in their midst;
- train their fears by seeking additional information and relationships with those they fear;
- renew their commitment to embracing the Other in obedience to God's instruction; and
- work to make their local church more welcoming of the Other.

Facilitating the Sessions

You do not need profound biblical understanding or expertise in political science and diversity to effectively facilitate dialogue on the material contained in *Fear of the Other*.

As a facilitator, your role is to

- understand the goals of the sessions;
- keep the group on task and moving forward;
- involve everyone in the meeting, including drawing out the quiet participants and reining in the domineering ones; and
- make sure that conversation stays respectful and productive especially during times of disagreement or uncomfortable discussions.

As you prepare for each episode it is good to be concerned that the sessions cover the material intended, that participants participate and interact, and that the elements needed for productive dialogue are present and supported.

In planning for a good class session, focus on the following areas:

- climate and environment
- logistics and room arrangements
- ground rules and a covenant

Climate and Environment

There are many factors that impact how safe and comfortable people feel about interacting with each other and participating. The environment and general "climate" of a group gathering sets an important tone for participation. Ensure to the best of your ability that meetings are taking place in a safe, accessible location and that the space can accommodate the group. Learn everyone's name and find ways to encourage participants to interact with one another.

Logistics and Room Arrangements

As a facilitator, the logistics of the meeting are something to consider, whether you're responsible for them or not. Having chairs in a circle or around a table as well as refreshments encourages discussion, equality, and familiarity. If possible, make sure you have newsprint or other board space to write on as well as an easel and markers. Also make sure you have available space to hang newsprint/flip chart paper (if you use it). Use name tags, especially if people do not know each other well. Lastly, computers, tablets, and/or smartphones can be used to enhance the experience, though some may find these to be a distraction.

Ground Rules and a Covenant

Talking about fears, especially fears of other people can be an uncomfortable and even embarrassing process. The need to build a safe and comfortable environment is essential given the material covered in *Fear of the Other*. Differing political and theological beliefs on subjects like immigration, racism, and Christian/Muslim relations can trigger active disagreement. As facilitator you have a few points to consider. How do you encourage those who are worried their ideas will be attacked or mocked to participate? How do you hold back the big talkers who tend to dominate while still making them feel good about their participation? Much of the answer lies in some basic ground rules or "road rules" (guidelines for your group's journey).

In the first session, one of the activities involves the group creating a covenant to make the group inviting and inclusive. Do not skip over this step. You will want to allow adequate time for this activity. Let the participants create their covenant rather than giving them one to follow. This builds a sense of empowerment in the participants and a much greater sense of investment in following the guidelines for healthy conversation. Here are some common ground rules in case the group seeks out ideas to get them started:

- Be on time.
- Respect each other.
- Let one person speak at a time.
- Listen to what other people are saying. (God's word often comes to us through others' thoughts and stories.)
- Do not mock or attack other people's ideas.

Helpful Hints

Because every group is different, your group will have its own set of dynamics and challenges. The following are some tips to help your group succeed.

Start and End the Meeting on Time

Start on time. Begin to acknowledge that the time to end the session is near about ten minutes ahead of time so that the conversation can move toward closure. Some leaders may offer to continue the conversation after the meeting ends, giving participants permission to leave.

Welcome Everyone

Make a point to welcome everyone who comes. Learn names and make sure that everyone has an opportunity to introduce themselves, especially in groups where the participants don't know one another.

Encourage Participation

This is an essential task for a facilitator. Encourage people to share their experiences and ideas, and urge those with relevant background information to share it at appropriate times. If participants seem restless or in a haze, you may need to take a break, or speed up or slow down the pace of the meeting. And if you see confused looks on too many faces, you may need to stop and check in with the group to make sure everyone knows where you are in the discussion and that the group is with you.

Be Flexible

Sometimes issues will arise in the meeting that are so important they will take much more time than you thought. You may have to alter your agenda to discuss them. Be sure to check with group about whether this is okay. Always give participants permission to leave at the scheduled ending time.

Be Aware of Your Own Behavior

The facilitator has an opportunity to model healthy dialogue by consistently using positive and respectful language, honoring the group's time, encouraging the open exchange of ideas, and affirming the gift of diversity within participant perspectives, experiences, and personal stories.

The Classroom Experience

Each session of *Fear of the Other* follows the same essential structure, with a suggested classroom length of sixty minutes. Groups with time to study ninety minutes or more may want to add eight to ten minutes or so to each of these.

Gathering (5–10 Minutes)

This time is for spiritual centering using a biblical text or other sacred text related to the theme of that chapter. It is an opportunity for the community to open in prayer and spiritual reflection.

Reflections on the Chapter (20 Minutes)

During this time the participants explore the key themes of the chapter and discuss their ideas about and experiences with those themes. A combination of small and large group reflection, activities that encourage personal reflection, and sharing are the centerpiece of this time.

Video Segment and Discussion Questions (25 Minutes)

Participants view the video segment with William H. Willimon, author of *Fear of the Other* and professor of the practice of Christian ministry at Duke University in Chapel Hill, North Carolina, and Delia Catalina Ramirez, deputy director of the Community Renewal Society in Chicago, Illinois. Before each video segment, the leader asks participants to listen for something (story, idea, etc.) that resonates with their own experience growing up or today. After the video, groups will choose to talk about one or more of the discussion questions.

Final Exercise and Closing Prayer (5–10 Minutes)

The final exercise is intended to support participants in finding practical applications for what they have discussed in their own lives and to commit to some sort of tangible action that will further their learning. It is also a time to encourage participants to prepare for the next week's session and to close in prayer.

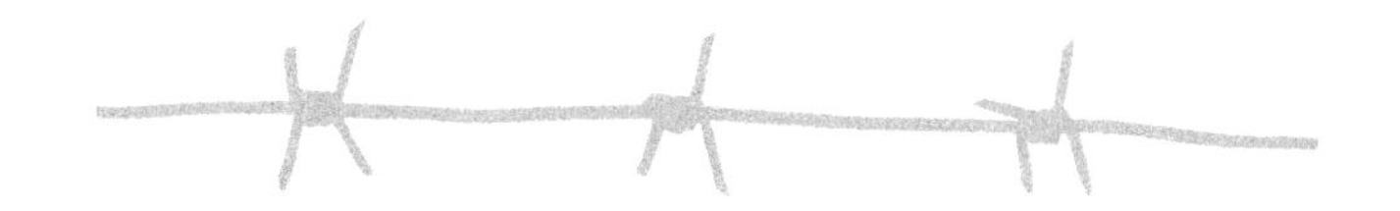

Introduction and Episode 1

SAVED BY THE OTHER

Introduction

Everyone has experienced Otherness at some point in their life. Some may have only one or two experiences of being regarded as different, an outsider, or looked down upon while others may have more stories about being the Other than they care to share. Sorting people into groups and then giving those groups labels (insider/outsider, majority/minority, citizen/foreigner) is a prevalent social practice. Usually it is the larger, more powerful group that determines the rules and rights for the treatment of the Others. This dynamic can be experienced in families, communities, churches, and businesses as well as in institutions like schools, the health care system, and the government.

As Christians we know that Christ died so that we could be reconciled to God and through God's grace move from Otherness to insider status in the family of God. And then Christ called us to show the same love shown to us by embracing the Others around us. So what keeps us from following Christ's command to love? While there is more than one answer to this question, one big reason is fear. The purpose of this small group study is to identify, reflect on, and deal with our fear of the Other so that we can be the disciples that Christ calls and expects us to be.

This opening session will help your class

1. share personal experiences of being the Other;
2. identify situations where fear of the Other is impacting relationships, communities, the church, and the world and apply a reading of 1 John 4:18 to these situations; and
3. commit together to create an environment of support, prayer, and trust.

Gathering (5–10 Minutes)

Invite participants to listen as you read aloud 1 John 4:16-21.

> God is love, and those who remain in love remain in God and God remains in them. This is how love has been perfected in us, so that we can have confidence on the Judgment Day, because we are exactly the same as God is in this world. There is no fear in love, but perfect love drives out fear, because fear expects punishment. The person who is afraid has not been made perfect in love. We love because God first loved us. If anyone says, I love God, and hates a brother or sister, he is a liar, because the person who doesn't love a brother or sister who can be seen can't love God, who can't be seen. This commandment we have from him: Those who claim to love God ought to love their brother and sister also.

Ask students to reflect quietly on those words for a few moments. After the silence, ask if someone is willing to share how they felt listening to those verses. What words, phrases, or ideas resonated with them or made them uncomfortable and why?

End the gathering time with a short prayer.

Reflections on the Chapter (20 Minutes)

There will be two rounds of sharing and discussion about the chapter (time permitting).

Round 1

Everyone will share one story about a time in his or her life when he or she felt like an outsider or considered him- or herself the Other. (Stories should not be more than a couple of minutes.) At the end of each story, ask the participant to share three words that describe what it was like for him or her to be the Other. Ideally, the words should be written somewhere that the whole group can see. After all participants have shared their story and their three words, the class will take a moment to reflect on the list of words that have been lifted up. Words like *lonely*, *angry*, *motivated*, *sad*, *frustrated* should be expected.

Round 2

Have the class brainstorm a list of situations where fear of the Other is impacting relationships, communities, the church, and the world and write them up where everyone can see. The list might include the global migrant/refugee crisis, Democrats versus Republicans, fear of church schism between conservatives and progressives, America building a wall on the Mexican border, LGBTQ rights, police and unarmed civilians of color, local ballot measures, and so on.

Invite the group to talk about how the words expressing the experiences of being the Other generated during round 1 might fit into the situations listed. For example, loneliness might be experienced by immigrants in an unfamiliar land. Political parties might feel frustrated about not having their ideas and preferences "win the day" as policies are made. Have the class break into smaller groups and select one of the listed situations and do the following:

1. Determine who the Other is in the situation and why.
2. Read 1 John 4:18, and apply it to this situation. What does it mean for perfect love to drive out fear in this situation? What action do you believe God might be asking us to take?

Invite the small groups to share their conclusions with the whole class.

Video Segment and Discussion Questions (25 Minutes)

Watch the video segment with William H. Willimon, author of *Fear of the Other* and professor of the practice of Christian ministry at Duke University in Chapel Hill, North Carolina, and Delia Catalina Ramirez, deputy director of the Community Renewal Society in Chicago, Illinois.

Before the video plays, ask participants to listen for something (story, idea, etc.) that resonates with their own experience growing up or today.

Choose one or more of the questions below to prompt discussion following the video.

1. What did you hear? What came to mind or stood out to you in this conversation?
2. Will Willimon says that Jesus was "resisted in great part because of his wide embrace of those considered outside the bounds." Can you recall anyone scandalized for this kind of wide embrace? Who were some of those outside the bounds of the insider groups where you grew up?

3. "All of us are immigrants to the Christian faith." What does that mean?

4. Willimon says he hopes people who participate in this study will join Jesus, who knocks down every barrier and wall to save the world. Does joining Jesus in the work of love excite or scare you (or both)? What do you hope to get out of this study (e.g., less fear/more love, a willingness to embrace and welcome outsiders, helping people you love to appreciate the image of God in others)?

Final Exercise and Closing Prayer (5–10 Minutes)

Now that the group has spent some time in discussion and forming community, they will create agreements for what it means to be a community of hospitality and embrace—especially for those with differing beliefs, opinions, and experiences. What will hospitality and embracing everyone in the group look like? What are we willing to be held accountable for? Examples might include praying for one another, listening to and considering other points of view, speaking in a respectful manner, encouraging honesty, respecting confidentiality, and so on.

Once the group has completed its list of community agreements, they should be printed and displayed for future sessions.

Remind the group to read chapter 2, "The Other, My Enemy," for next week's discussion.

Invite someone to close the session with prayer.

Episode 2

THE OTHER, MY ENEMY

Introduction

Fear is a very human response. It not only influences our behavior but is hardwired into our brains. Despite our natural tendencies to respond to fear with force and judgment or flight and suppression, we do have a choice of how to respond when fear—especially fear of the Other—grips us.

This session will help your class

1. explore the definition of *xenophobia* and modern-day examples of it;
2. identify and examine the groups that illicit feelings of fear within participants; and
3. learn how to train our fears so that as Christians, we can connect to those "strangers" whom God is calling us to embrace.

Gathering (5–10 Minutes)

Invite participants to listen as you read aloud Leviticus 19:33-34.

> When immigrants live in your land with you, you must not cheat them. Any immigrant who lives with you must be treated as if they were one of your citizens. You must love them as yourself, because you were immigrants in the land of Egypt; I am the LORD your God.

Ask students to reflect quietly on those words for a minute or two. After the silence, tell them that a foreigner, stranger, or immigrant doesn't always mean a person moving from one country to another (the original message of this passage). One can feel like a foreigner or stranger whenever encountering new and different experiences, technologies, groups, cultures, or unfamiliar territories. Then have them turn to a person next to them and share their reflections after listening to the command to Israel about how to treat those who are foreign to us. What words, phrases, or ideas resonate with them?

End the gathering time with a word of prayer.

Reflections on the Chapter (20 Minutes)

Share with the class that *xenophobia* comes from the Greek word (*xenoi*) for strangers. The Miriam-Webster Dictionary defines *xenophobia* as "a fear or hatred of strangers or foreigners or of anything that is strange or foreign."[1]

Invite the class come up with a list of groups that appear to be feared or hated in today's society. Write the list where everyone can see. Then ask participants to identify some of the reasons that each group is feared and write those as well.

Ask the group to discuss the following questions:

1. *Merriam-Webster*, s.v. "xenophobia," accessed June 22, 2017, https://www.merriam-webster.com/dictionary/xenophobia.

- What do you feel looking at the list and the qualifiers that have been listed and why?
- Where do the reasons for fearing these groups come from?
- Are there reasons for fear listed that you feel are exaggerated or inaccurate?
- Do any of the reasons listed escalate fear and anxiety about a group?
- What alternative narratives about these groups might be offered to put these fears into perspective?

Video Segment and Discussion Questions (25 Minutes)

Watch the video segment with William H. Willimon, author of *Fear of the Other* and professor of the practice of Christian ministry at Duke University in Chapel Hill, North Carolina, and Delia Catalina Ramirez, deputy director of the Community Renewal Society in Chicago, Illinois.

Before the video plays, ask participants to listen for something (story, idea, etc.) that resonates with their own experience growing up or today. Choose one or more of the questions below to prompt discussion following the video.

1. What did you hear? What came to mind or stood out to you in this conversation?
2. How is fear a gift? List examples. Have you ever known someone with no healthy fear of danger?
3. In the video Willimon says that "part of growing up is not only learning the right fears and what to fear rightly . . . but also learning how to control our fears." Has anyone ever helped you retrain your own disproportionate fear of some-

thing (e.g., swimming, heights, math, speaking in public)? Share that story.

4. Our "fears are conquered . . . not so much through better ideas but by actually living encounters," says Will Willimon. Is this true? Have you or someone you know been helped with an unrealistic fear?

Final Exercise (5–10 Minutes)

Remind the group that many of our fears come from direct experiences or from information we get from others (family, friends, news sources). When we generalize our fears and use them to judge an entire group we move away from God's command to love the stranger. One way to combat our fear of the Other is to look for new and different perspectives, experiences, and information that can broaden our understanding and enrich our lives.

Invite the class to break up into groups of three and share one or two things that they can do in the coming week to gain a different perspective about the Other that they fear.

Remind the group to read chapter 3, "Learning to Fear Like Christians," for next week's discussion.

Invite someone to close the session with prayer.

Episode 3

LEARNING TO FEAR LIKE CHRISTIANS

Introduction

It is tempting for Christians to use theological beliefs and biblical interpretations to justify fear and exclusion of the Other. Our faith, however, requires us to see the Other as loved and cherished by God no matter their race, age, religion, or any other social classification.

This session will help your class

1. examine how Christians are called to respond to the Other;
2. explore the idea that when Christians choose to exclude they "fear the Other more than they fear God"; and
3. identify ways to live the steps of embrace (opening, waiting, closing and opening again) in everyday life.

Gathering (5–10 Minutes)

Invite participants to listen as you read aloud a verse from the hymn "Amazing Grace" by John Newton.

'Twas grace that taught my heart to fear,
and grace my fears relieved;
how precious did that grace appear
the hour I first believed.

Ask students to reflect quietly on those words for a minute or two. After the silence have them turn to a person next to them to share what words, phrases, or ideas resonate with them.

End the gathering time with a word of prayer.

Reflections on the Chapter (20 Minutes)

Invite the class to break up into three groups, and have each group reflect together on one of the following quotes by Bishop Willimon in chapter 3 of *Fear of the Other*:

- "Our problem, in regard to fear, is that we fear the Other more than we fear the God who commands, 'Love each other'" (p. 39).
- "Judgments can be made against evil done by another, but Christians make those judgments with confession of the possibility of our own complicity in the sinful acts that we condemn, with differentiation between the perpetrator as a person (that is, a dearly loved child of God), and his or her wrong actions that are an offense against God and neighbor" (p. 42).
- "As Dietrich Bonhoeffer said, love in action is so much more significant than 'love in our dreams'" (p. 57).

Ask each group to describe the meaning of these statements, perhaps restating the meaning in their own words. Then have each group share their explanations with the other two.

When all the groups have shared, ask the whole gathering to reflect together on these questions:

- What are the obstacles that prevent Christians from loving the Other when Jesus so clearly commands us to do so?
- What can we do to overcome these obstacles?

Video Segment and Discussion Questions (25 Minutes)

Watch the video segment with William H. Willimon, author of *Fear of the Other* and professor of the practice of Christian ministry at Duke University in Chapel Hill, North Carolina, and Delia Catalina Ramirez, deputy director of the Community Renewal Society in Chicago, Illinois.

Before the video plays, ask participants to listen for something (story, idea, etc.) that resonates with their own experience growing up or today. Choose one or more of the questions below to prompt discussion following the video.

1. What did you hear? What came to mind or stood out to you in this conversation?
2. Bishop Willimon says, "We should be fearful of disappointing God, of betraying ourselves and our values and goals." Is a healthy fear of God passé or out of fashion in our culture? How is that both good and not so good? What is the difference between being terrified of God and a healthy awe and fear of failing to heed Jesus's call to love?
3. Christians confess their sins (tell the truth about what we've done wrong and the good we've left undone). How important is naming our own family history of xenophobia

and exclusion? Does the church create spaces where this is practiced openly (without undue shame)?

4. How/why is faith always more (but not less) than a "personal relationship," more than just "me and Jesus"? Can God make us holy (truly loving) in this life?

Final Exercise (5–10 Minutes)

Share with the group that on pages 45–46, the steps of embracing someone are described. First the arms open as a sign of vulnerability and willingness to relate differently. Then there is a time of waiting and allowing the possibility of response. This is followed by closing the arms and bringing the Other closer in relationship. Finally the arms open again releasing the Other to live, accompanied by our love and respect. While it is not always appropriate or possible to physically embrace one whom we fear or who is unfamiliar to us, we are nevertheless called to embrace.

Invite the group to think about an Other who elicits feelings of fear and/or judgment. Examples could include a racial or ethnic group, a religious group, people from a certain country, the executives at your place of work, members of certain group in your church, and so on. Have participants work in pairs, with each person identifying and sharing with their partner practical ways that could lead to the steps of embracing that Other (opening, waiting, closing and opening again).

This does not mean that they have to take the steps with a specific person although they are free to do that. For example, if young black men are the Other then some steps might be to watch videos on Youtube or find and read articles about young black men doing positive things (open), posting a positive comment about the video or article (waiting), sharing the video or article with friends or family along with your thoughts about how it impacted you (closing), praying for the safety of young black men who are often misjudged and labeled as being threatening and violent (opening). Here is another example of taking the steps of embrace with an actual person; in this case the Other is a homeless person: start a conversation (opening), look them in the eye (waiting), give them money or food (closing), and say, "God bless you" as you depart their presence (opening).

The goal is to not only take the steps of embrace but to notice the impact they have on you.

Remind the group to read chapter 4, "Loving the Other in Church," for next week's discussion.

Invite someone to close the session with prayer.

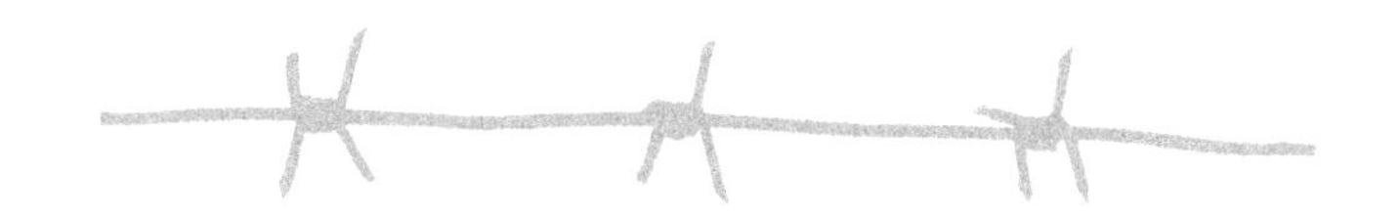

Episode 4

LOVING THE OTHER IN CHURCH

Introduction

The role of the church is to welcome the Other and show hospitality as a visible sign of God's determination to love all people. Too often, focus is placed on serving the people inside the congregation when in fact Christ is calling the people inside to serve the people outside. Church members can become so focused on themselves and their own needs that they forget that the way of Christ always leads to the Other.

This session will help your class

1. redefine the role of the church from being inwardly focused to being outwardly focused;
2. explore what it means to receive the Other; and
3. consider ways to make the church more welcoming and hospitable.

Gathering (5–10 Minutes)

Invite participants to listen as you read aloud Acts 2:1-12.

> When Pentecost Day arrived, they were all together in one place. Suddenly a sound from heaven like the howling of a fierce wind filled the entire house where they were sitting. They saw what seemed to be individual flames of fire alighting on each one of them. They were all filled with the Holy Spirit and began to speak in other languages as the Spirit enabled them to speak.
>
> There were pious Jews from every nation under heaven living in Jerusalem. When they heard this sound, a crowd gathered. They were mystified because everyone heard them speaking in their native languages. They were surprised and amazed, saying, "Look, aren't all the people who are speaking Galileans, every one of them? How then can each of us hear them speaking in our native language? Parthians, Medes, and Elamites; as well as residents of Mesopotamia, Judea, and Cappadocia, Pontus and Asia, Phrygia and Pamphylia, Egypt and the regions of Libya bordering Cyrene; and visitors from Rome (both Jews and converts to Judaism), Cretans and Arabs—we hear them declaring the mighty works of God in our own languages!" They were all surprised and bewildered. Some asked each other, "What does this mean?"

Ask students to reflect quietly on those words for a minute or two. After the silence have them turn to a person next to them to share what words, phrases, or ideas resonate with them.

End the gathering time with a word of prayer.

Reflections on the Chapter (20 Minutes)

Invite participants to break into twos and threes and reflect on the following questions:

- Who are the Others in the community surrounding your church—those who are different or unfamiliar in some way?

- What would the people in the local community say about your church? How would they describe the people?
- What are the ways in which your church received the Other? How are they welcomed and included?

Have them share highlights from their conversation with the whole group. Then invite them to come back together and think about the qualities of a welcoming and hospitable church. Ask the participants to brainstorm all of the things that they believe a welcoming congregation would do. List them for everyone to see.

Invite the group to think once again about the others in the community surrounding the church and ponder how they might experience the list of qualities and activities of a welcoming congregation. When thought of from the perspective of the Other, do those activities still feel welcoming? Sometimes churches learn a hard lesson when they realize that the things that seem welcoming to people within the congregation are not experienced as welcoming to people outside of the congregation.

Video Segment and Discussion Questions (25 Minutes)

Watch the video segment with William H. Willimon, author of *Fear of the Other* and professor of the practice of Christian ministry at Duke University in Chapel Hill, North Carolina, and Delia Catalina Ramirez, deputy director of the Community Renewal Society in Chicago, Illinois.

Before the video plays, ask participants to listen for something (story, idea, etc.) that resonates with their own experience growing up or today. Choose one or more of the questions below to prompt discussion following the video.

1. What did you hear? What came to mind or stood out to you in this conversation?
2. Willimon says, "When a church becomes inner focused on its needs and its current membership . . . it dies—it just kind of seems to be a divine law." Do you agree? Have you seen this happen to churches? How do we keep church from becoming a "self-improvement society"?
3. "The church is where you come to be enlisted by God into responsibility, concern for Others." If this is true, what must we do?
4. What is God calling us to give up if we are going to live responsibly as the hands and feet of Jesus in the world (e.g., warm notions that our parents/churches weren't wrong in their prejudices, the stability of our privileged place, an inflated sense of being right or God's chosen)?
5. What is a "hermeneutic of hospitality"? (Hint: the charitable fallback position of Christians in any encounter with Otherness [i.e., look for the good, appreciate their struggles, find things you share in common].)

Final Exercise (5–10 Minutes)

Look at the list of ideas for welcoming and receiving strangers on pages 79–81 in *Fear of the Other*. Invite the group to break up into pairs and together pick the three ideas that most resonate with them. Each pair will get an opportunity to share the ideas they selected with the group and why.

Remind the group to read chapter 5, "Jesus, the Other," for next week's discussion.

Invite someone to close the session with prayer.

Episode 5

JESUS, THE OTHER

Introduction

Throughout Jesus's ministry, he constantly encourages those he encounters to "fear not" while simultaneously extending the hand of love, forgiveness, healing, and compassion to the Others that were most feared and despised in society. In doing so, he became the Other who was tortured and killed due to the very human tendency to fear and act on the fear of the Other.

As modern-day disciples of Jesus we are reminded that our task is not to simply reach out, love and serve the Other, but to allow the Other to transform our hearts, minds, and actions—to save us from our fear-filled selves, just as Jesus has saved us from sin.

This session will help your class

1. reimagine the relationship between neighbors;
2. explore what it means to see Jesus in the Other; and
3. reflect on learnings over the last five sessions and encourage each other for the journey ahead.

Gathering (10 Minutes)

Invite participants to listen as you read aloud Luke 10:25-37.

A legal expert stood up to test Jesus. "Teacher," he said, "what must I do to gain eternal life?"

Jesus replied, "What is written in the Law? How do you interpret it?"

He responded, "You must love the Lord your God with all your heart, with all your being, with all your strength, and with all your mind, and love your neighbor as yourself."

Jesus said to him, "You have answered correctly. Do this and you will live."

But the legal expert wanted to prove that he was right, so he said to Jesus, "And who is my neighbor?"

Jesus replied, "A man went down from Jerusalem to Jericho. He encountered thieves, who stripped him naked, beat him up, and left him near death. Now it just so happened that a priest was also going down the same road. When he saw the injured man, he crossed over to the other side of the road and went on his way. Likewise, a Levite came by that spot, saw the injured man, and crossed over to the other side of the road and went on his way. A Samaritan, who was on a journey, came to where the man was. But when he saw him, he was moved with compassion. The Samaritan went to him and bandaged his wounds, tending them with oil and wine. Then he placed the wounded man on his own donkey, took him to an inn, and took care of him. The next day, he took two full days' worth of wages and gave them to the innkeeper. He said, 'Take care of him, and when I return, I will pay you back for any additional costs.' What do you think? Which one of these three was a neighbor to the man who encountered thieves?"

Then the legal expert said, "The one who demonstrated mercy toward him."

Jesus told him, "Go and do likewise."

Invite participants to reflect silently on those words for two minutes. After the silence, have them turn to a person next to them to share what words, phrases, or ideas resonate with them.

End the gathering time with a word of prayer.

Reflections on the Chapter (20 Minutes)

Invite the group to identify the neighbors that their church has the possibility of serving.

Write the list up where everyone can see. Then have the group split into groups of three and select one of the neighbors listed. Each group will create two lists related to the neighbors they selected:

1. ways that the church can serve those neighbors; and
2. gifts that those neighbors have to share with the church.

Have each group report the neighbors that they selected and their two lists. Spend a few minutes inviting reflections about what has been shared. Then have the class discuss as a whole group the following question: what gets revealed when we see Jesus the outcast in the neighbors we overlook, ignore, or avoid?

Video Segment and Discussion Questions (25 Minutes)

Watch the video segment with William H. Willimon, author of *Fear of the Other* and professor of the practice of Christian ministry at Duke University in Chapel Hill, North Carolina, and Delia Catalina Ramirez, deputy director of the Community Renewal Society in Chicago, Illinois.

Before the video plays, ask participants to listen for something (story, idea, etc.) that resonates with their own experience growing up or today. Choose one or more of the questions below to prompt discussion following the video.

1. What did you hear? What came to mind or stood out to you in this conversation?

2. The pastor in Willimon's story about the Jesus Rave says that many young people are angry at their parents and people who look like Will for not keeping their promises. What did she mean by that? How might that change the way we think of people outside our "church-y" boundaries? Could they be closer to God than we are?

3. Christians are missionaries (those called to cross boundaries with the good news of Jesus's love). What are some of the human-concocted borders that we are called to cross (e.g., race, class, age, culture, denomination)?

4. "The church is God's answer to what's wrong with the world." How could moving from fear to love make your church God's answer to some of the ills in your community?

Final Exercise (5–10 Minutes)

Invite the class to think about all that has been discussed over the last five sessions. Open the space for participants to share the one learning or take-away that has most impacted them. Then have class members turn to a partner and share some ways that they will let their love of God and commitment to the command of Christ to love our neighbors override their fear of the Other in their lives moving forward. Invite partners to close their sharing time by praying for one another as they take their commitment to love God and neighbor out into the world.

Call the class back together. Go around the circle and invite each participant to share one word that captures this learning experience with *Fear of the Other*.

Invite someone to close the session with prayer.

CPSIA information can be obtained
at www.ICGtesting.com
Printed in the USA
LVOW02s0403170717
541307LV00007B/8/P